Someone To Love the Little Girl in Me

"The Silent Scream Series"
Part I

Someone to Love the Little Girl in Me

Yolanda Lee~George

While the publisher has made every attempt to release correct addresses and contact information at the time of this publication, the publisher assumes no responsibility for errors or changes that come about after the publish date.

All rights reserved. No part of this book may be reproduced, scanned, or distributed in any printed or electronic forms existing now or in the future without written permission from the publisher. For information regarding permission, please write to:

Black~Butterfly Publishing

Please help in the fight against piracy of copyrighted materials. Purchase only authorized editions.

ISBN: 978-0-9910760-1-7 © 2013

Black~Butterfly Publishing Inc.

All rights reserved. Published 2011.

Printed in the United States of America.

Autograph Page

Acknowledgements

I want to first thank **Jesus Christ,** who is the head of my life in all things for without **HIM** this would not be happening. The Lord allowed my childhood test to be my adult testimony. I want to thank my dad **Raymond Lee Sr.** for loving me unconditionally from birth, and supporting me through my choice to do this book, even though we both knew it would open some bandaged wounds. I want to thank my children **Nijah, Johnna, Johntavia, Johnavia and John** III for not being ashamed of me as I put this book out, knowing that it would air the dirty laundry of my past. Thanks to my mother **Patricia Lee** because without you, I would not be the strong and independent woman I am today. Thank you **Sabrina Chandler** for always loving and standing by me, and constantly pushing and believing in me. You said I would make this happen, and you were right. Thanks to **Ann Stanback**, you know that you've loved me from childhood, you were my strength on those trying days, and been there through some childhood tears, and I love you so much, my sister **Valerie Lee-Jackson** for loving me this day and the closeness that we now share (thank you God), **Felicia Lee** for encouraging me and ALWAYS loving me, to **Donna Ashby,** my crazy baby sister whom I love so much, also, to my entire extended family for showing me so much love when I wanted to hide away from the rest of the world, to my cousin **Vondalyn "Fuggie" Bryant,** you don't realize how much you helped me towards the end of this book because I was feeling a little down and unsure, thank you cousin for all your support I love you girl.

ADDITION PHASE II

To my husband **Lorenzo George, Sr**, baby thank you thank you thank you for loving me through all of my pains, loving me when I didn't truly love myself, loving me when I tried to run you off, loving me while I aired my dirty laundry, loving me while I put in time to revise this book, for just loving me from your heart **THANK YOU FOR LOVING THE LITTLE GIRL IN ME!**

Special Thanks to:

Maurice Gardner, for taking such lovely photo's that turned out to be my book cover, you are the best! To *Darlene Brown,* you are gone but not forgotten. You taught me about my hygiene, and that was something very important in my life at thirteen years old. I don't know where I would have been without you. My spiritual **mother, Eddie Mae Gooden,** (who went to be with the Lord February 2013) thank you for the anointing oil and praying in the Holy Ghost for me when I had no clue what you were doing and wished some days you'd leave me alone, thank you for never giving up on me and praying for me, I love you mommy R.I.P. To **Cilicia Prince,** I thank GOD for bringing you into my life C.C., you have no clue how I appreciate how you've filled my life in such a short time, and I love you so much. Thanks to **Amber Lamar** for being right there beside me and making this day happen for me. **Also thanks to Dawn McConnell** for allowing me to aggravate you every second about this book and for pointing me to my lovely editor **Attorney Grace Yang.**

Thanks to **Pastor Rashidi Collins** for believing in me, still praying for me and speaking prophetic volume into my life, knowing that God has a plan for me even when I don't see it at times, I love you Pastor Collins! To my Victory Tabernacle UPC family – especially **Sis. Shawn Saxton, Sabrina Saxton,**

Sis. Thompson for that special kind of love that only you know how to give me! Thank you **Georgette Gunn,** my sister, my running partner, my ACE, my everything; we've certainly shared so much together, my ride-or-die chick lol! Thank you for loving me unto this day even if we don't hear from each other for lengths at a time, we are still so connected in many ways. I love you G.G. for life. I do thank everyone for your support on this book and for all the future books to come. **Prophetess Pastor Kimberly Brown**, I thank God for allowing our paths to cross, I thank God for the Prophetic anointing that is on your life. You told me "through God" that I wasn't finished yet and I receive it in the Name of Jesus, you said God is about to elevate me to a new dimension. I thank you for your obedience and telling me what "Thus said the Lord". I love you!

FOREWORD

by Pastor Rashidi Collins of Victory Tabernacle U.P.C.

Luke 8:11 – Now the parable is this: The seed is the Word of God.

John 6:63b – The words that I speak unto you, they are spirit, and they are life.

Seeds are amazing specimens of nature. It is incredible that contained within every seed is the blueprint for self perpetuation. A tiny seed can potentially yield limitless returns. While this can be considered quite positive the question has to be asked, "What if the seed has a negative dimension?" The scriptures argue that words are seeds. Good seeds produce good fruit and bad seeds yield bad fruit. In like manner, positive words produce positive behavior and negative words engender negative results. Words are the vehicles through which spirits are transferred. Perverse words planted in the mind of a child attract dark forces that attempt to dictate the destiny of the soul. Two realities are revealed by the words of Jesus that are quoted above: (1) Words are seeds and (2) Within every word there is a spiritual possibility. With these principles in mind, one should approach the reading of this work with the understanding that a myriad of negative seeds were planted in the author's life at a very early stage. Set against the backdrop of maternal scorn, perverse environments and over exposure to lascivious behavior, the mind of the young woman telling this story was filled with imagery that was designed to facilitate her destruction. Many of the decisions that were made by Yolanda Lee were influenced by the spiritual harvest that manifested in her life as a result of the seeds that were sown by those who should have protected her from evil influences.

One might argue that individuals have freedom of choice and they can alter their course in life if they decide to do so. Agreed! This is why the story you are about to read is a remarkable tale of emerging from the clutches of the devil by cultivating the right seeds in one's spiritual garden. God is in the business of planting seeds. Satan is in the same business. Who's working on your field?

....

Table of Contents

Chapter 1– Sometimes I Feel Like A Motherless Child

Chapter 2 -Welcome Into Purity, Little Manifested Spirits

Chapter 3 -Oh What An Ugly Jealous Little Girl You Are

Chapter 4 – I Love My Mommy Dearest

Chapter 5 - Darlene To the Rescue

Chapter 6 - Hard Working Man

Chapter 7–What's Done In the Dark Will Come to the Light!

Chapter 8 -Giving Up The Cherry Pop or Did I?

Chapter 9 -Starting to Find My Own Wild Child Identity

Chapter 10 – Let's Party and Have More Sex

Chapter 11 - You're So Devilish

Chapter 12 - Pimps, Hoe's, Sex, Drugs, and Loving It!

Chapter 13 – Look At Me, I'm Important, I'm Somebody Now!

Chapter 14 -The Girl Got A Little Talent To!

Chapter 15 -The Word of God Will Always Follow You Little Girl!

Table of Contents

Chapter 16 – Choosy Lover

Chapter 17 -Ouch Was That A Spirit Speaking Out From The Past?

Chapter 18 - Just Where Do You Think You're Going!

Chapter 19 – Back to Those Familiar Spirits, Didn't See It Coming

Chapter 20 - You're About to be a Mother

Chapter 21 - You're a Lying Wonder, You Never Loved Me, You Lusted Me!

Chapter 22–Now You're the Mother of Two and Still Messed Up!

Chapter 23 - Time to do Something Different and Still Do My Thing

Chapter 24 - I Need Some Attention, So I Guess I'll Dance!

Chapter 25 – Seeking Out My Victims!

Chapter 26 - Family Secrets AGAIN

Chapter 27 - Let's Have More Fun

Chapter 28 –Girl You Still Live Dangerously

Chapter 29 -Same Ole Games Man, Come On!

To My Readers:

Sometimes the life that we live growing up will cause us to make bad choices later in life. It may cause us to reach for things to fill voids for what we didn't get growing up, but only GOD can truly fill those voids, so here we go! This book is about me working towards my own healing process. I realize that other people may read it and not like what I have written, or agree with me, but this is my story. It is not meant to paint an ugly picture of my family, or try to make one parent appear to have been better than the other, because I learned some very valuable lessons from both of them. Although I do mention my family, this book is not about what they did, but more about how I interacted with them, and how it shaped my life growing up. I don't get into their personal lives or their individual battles because that's their story. My main focus was sharing my experiences with you and telling you about my own **SILENT SCREAMS.** These events and interactions are what shaped my life going from childhood into adulthood. In the end, I just really needed and wanted for **"Someone to Love the Little Girl in Me."**

-Author Yolanda V. Lee~George

Chapter 1 – *Sometimes I Feel Like A Motherless Child*

I feel like I was always searching for someone to love me, growing up in a house where there was no love shown, no affection expressed, and no really special moments to think about. My dad did try to do his best when he made it possible for us to go to Silver Spring, Six Gun Territory every year for vacation, but even then there was no happiness between my parents. I never heard the words "I love you in my house growing up." My dad worked all of the time to provide for us, but after working so much, he did not have much time left to give. My dad worked so that my mother could stay home and raise the kids and take care of the household. It wasn't like he forced her into this role; this was a choice that they made. My mom was a different story; she was frigid emotionally and didn't show love. She did take care of me as far as keeping my hair combed, making sure I had clean clothes, even if they were hand me downs from my sister. I'm sure someone may be saying "So what more did you want from her?" What I wanted more than anything was to feel a *"mother's love."* I wanted her nurturing, I wanted her to laugh with me, I wanted for her to tell me that I was pretty, and I wanted to see her smile at me the way she smiled at my sister. There are some people that may have been around us, who may disagree with me, but they didn't know what went on behind closed doors. Some people came around after the damage had already started and I had already learned to hide my hurt and laugh it off. (*SILENT SCREAMS*) They really didn't know the truth, they didn't know that my mother was always cruel to me, and I never felt any love from her. My god-sister Eula would always say that momma loved us both the same, and that it was just me being mean. What she didn't realize was the root cause of me being that way. I never told her because she's a very outspoken person, and she would have gone straight to my mom to talk to her about it. She is the type of person that likes to make everything right if she can. The last thing a person could do was to try to make something right that my mom didn't feel was wrong. I'm sure that had Eula tried to question her about this, she would probably whipped my butt for telling. For the record, I think I was mean because I had been holding everything in and it showed on my face.

When we had family reunions or any kind of gathering, she'd introduce me as the mean one, or the one that didn't care about anything, but that wasn't true. I wasn't mean, things did hurt me, but I did as my dad told me. He said "Hold it in, and don't let the devil see you sweat or cry." I tried to do that, but I didn't know where my outlet was so I guess it did show on my face more than I realized. The thing that no one knew was that I cried almost every night silently to myself. (***SILENT SCREAMS***) I soaked my pillow with tears and held my mouth so my sister wouldn't hear me, because we all slept in the same bed.

We had an Uncle named Jimmy that came by every time he was in town and he genuinely loved us and cared about our education. Every time he'd come around he'd ask us about school. For the most part my sister and brothers hated when he talked to us about school. I guess it didn't bother me to much because I had someone to talk to me. My uncle always wanted what was best for us and I appreciated that and enjoyed talking to him. It actually made me feel smart!

Nevertheless, my mother would frequently tell me that I was dumb, stupid, and ignorant like my dad. She said that I would never amount to anything, and that no one would ever want me. She told me that I was black and ugly and would call me evil and it hurt tremendously. She made sure that all of the kids went to Sunday school and stayed for church, and would always dress us up real pretty, and for that I'm grateful because it's a reflection of my life today. She would have us ready for the young lady to pick us up because my mom didn't go to church with us.

Growing up, we would go to Plant City to visit my grandparents on both my dad and mom's side, and depending on whose house we were at, that's who we'd go to church with. My dad's family was Methodist and my mom's was Baptist. My great-grandmother "Grandma Bell," was a strong woman of God. She would pin a rose from her garden on us and we'd walk around the yard and she'd sing and read the bible to us. I was excited every time I knew we'd be going to see her because I enjoyed being a member of her backyard church. The words of the bible were so important to me when she read them. (I didn't realize that she was speaking the word into my spirit as a child).

Chapter 2 – *Welcome Into Purity, Little Manifested Spirits*

As a child, I saw so much cheating in my family. One particular individual cheated with just about any and every male friend or family member that would come around. I saw many things that people obviously didn't think that my little mind would be able to remember, but I did. I'd see friends and family come together, with everyone hugging, and then some of them would act like they were going to the store or some other place, but really, they were going to meet certain individuals and have sex, and everyone would meet back at the house as if nothing had happened.

Although I loved my dad like crazy, my take on men were that they were no good. I was just a kid but in my subconscious mind, I felt like men were just nasty. I knew they had wives, just like the women had husbands, but I don't think they really understood that you could not have sex in front of child and act as if it would not have any lasting effects on them. Now I didn't really understand what sex was at that age, but I knew that they were sneaking around doing something they should not be doing, and it wasn't some type of game. I saw her doing the same things, while making the same sounds with other men, so I wasn't sure who the person was that should've been having her make those sounds. So I believed that it must have been OK for her to take off her clothes and lay in the bed with all of them. As I sat there watching, I felt just like one of the paintings on the wall, or a piece of furniture, like I was there, but not really there. Sometimes I wondered if they were looking at me, so I didn't like those men coming around me at all, but I was told to get their money that they were handing me, and that I wasn't supposed to tell anyone where the money came from. I would roll my eyes at them. (I had the sex spirit jumping all over me and no one including me realized it).

I can't recall any friend or family member that wasn't a part of sleeping with this individual and paying her for it. I never understood why she was doing this until much later on in life. I found out that she was doing it out of hatred and for revenge. I didn't know that my little eyes, mind, heart and spirit was picking up these actions, and it found a way into my life at that early age, only to be realized as I grew older. As a child, I observed everything closely. I saw the lies; the sex, the money, and the family, all come together in one big ball of mess.

Chapter 3 – *Oh What An Ugly Jealous Little Girl You Are*

As time went on and I got older, I grew jealous of my sister because my mom worshiped her. I desperately wanted the attention that my mom gave to my sister. There is nothing like a mother's love, and she never gave it to me. I would simply cling to my dad whenever he was around. He was the breadwinner in the house providing security and showing his dedication and love daily.

My sister and I shared a volatile relationship. I had always thought of her as being very pretty and I envied that fact, and wanted to be her. She had friends, boyfriends, fun, jewelry and was popular, all the things that I wanted. She seemed to be something special to so many people. Despite my obvious admiration of her, she disliked me. She would tell me that I was ugly and there were times when people saw us out, and would make the comment that we looked alike, she would become infuriated and tell people not to say that. She took this so seriously that it affected the schools I attended. I went to Tampa Bay Technical School for the first year and a half of high school because she didn't want me to go to Leto High School with her. In the middle of my eleventh-grade year I transferred to Leto High because I really didn't have any friends at Tampa Bay Tech. I just felt uncomfortable there, even though I was always a loner, I just wanted a change, and she hated me for that. She instructed me not to talk to her in the hallway, and to most definitely not talk to her friends. She just wanted me to leave her alone. When I walked through the hallways, people would ask her if I was her sister and comment that I was pretty, or that I looked like her, and this only added fuel her anger. One of her friends asked her one day why she was so mean to me, but she did not give her an answer. When she saw me approaching her in the hallway at school, she would leave or just go the other way so she didn't have to deal with me. I pretended like it didn't hurt, but it hurt enormously because I loved my sister. I looked up to her so much even as my mom continued to praise her, and never giving me anything but admonishment.

 I also had two older brothers and a little cousin who my parents were raising as well. My mom even cherished her over me as well. I was not alone however; my oldest brother was treated very badly as well. I hurt for him at times because of the way my mom treated him. She would wait until she had company and embarrass him so badly in front of everyone. Sometimes she would wait until he got in the bath tub and then she would beat him with the broom or whatever she could get her hands on. It was if she hated him for whatever mistakes or hurts that was caused in her own life.

She always told him that he would never be anything. He would cry at night, thinking no one heard him, but I did, and I was silently crying along with him.

It was so hard watching the way she treated him when my dad was not around. She would always tell him that he was useless. My middle brother didn't have it so bad at that time because even as a child, he was always a hustler. He would sell bottles; recycle cans, or cut grass to make sure he had money in his pocket. I had another brother who was the oldest, but he did not live with us. He was my dad's son from a previous relationship, and he'd come on the weekends to stay with us sometimes. I never could understand what it was inside of people to make them belittle others and be so cold-hearted, but I remember that my grandmother on my mother's side was just like that as well. My best guess was that they had hidden hurt, and it came out that way towards others who may not have been the cause, but they were conveniently available to be the receiver of their outlet of pain. Some people, like my great-grandmother, must have known how to handle things because she was the best woman in the world to all of us.

Chapter 4 - *I Love My Mommy Dearest*

After so many years, you would think that age or circumstance would have changed a person, but my mom is still the same to this day. I remember back to the weekends when she'd make us breakfast; I'd watch my mom because I loved to watch her cook. I get all of my cooking skills from her, but my sister never cared about cooking; she always had other things to keep her occupied which was friends and fame. After we ate, we would get on the floor in the living room and watch TV together. We would laugh at the shows, and sometimes my dad would sit with us as well. There were also those special times when my dad would let us go to work with him. My brothers would help him at night in the store, and I would sit on the carpet and watch them until I would fall asleep. Other than that, I was mainly in the house or with Lisa, my childhood best friend. Lisa and I hung together all the time; she was my partner in crime.

There were days when my mom would talk mean to me, and call me stupid, dumb, mean, or just black and ugly. I would go outside and climb the big tree that was in our yard to the very top, and no one knew I was there. I would just sit up there and cry to myself. I was still trying to hold everything in, but there were so many silent screams going on inside of me until I didn't know what I was feeling some days. I was screaming silently and had cried so many hidden tears.

When my mom was around people, she would call me "Abby" making reference to the girl in the movie that was about a young girl who was possessed by the devil. She said that I reminded her of that character because I was nothing but pure mean. It wasn't that I was mean; I just used anger as my hiding place, where no one bothered me. It was the place where people didn't talk down to me, or ridicule me, but it was lonely in that place, and not where I wanted to be. My mom called me names for so long that I just I felt ugly. I didn't feel like I had a purpose for being alive. I didn't want to be around other people because I felt like everyone would either pick on me, or start laughing at me because I was ugly. I even had to get a weekly shot at the age of 10 for migraines. When we were younger my mom had us in an aerobic studio called Jackie's Studio. I've always been very limber and liked to do gymnastics, so she got us into the aerobics. I knew how to do many of the twist and turns that my sister couldn't do, and wanted to show something that I could do better than her, but my mom would rarely come in to watch. She would always be around the other side of the studio watching my sister. Because of our age difference, we weren't in the same group. Around that time, my sister was also a cheerleader, and I wanted to be one as well. It seemed to be so much fun, and she was popular at school, but my mom didn't let me cheer right away.

Family life started to change as we got older. My oldest brother dropped out of school because he started failing so much in class. He said that he just wasn't capable of doing good in school. He dropped out with scholarships waiting for him in basketball and football. After he dropped out, my mom told him that he couldn't stay there anymore since he didn't go to school. She said that he would either have to go back to school or go to the military, so he enlisted in the military, and that's where his real troubles began. My mother had made it her business to tell him all his life that she didn't think he was worth anything, so at first, he felt he wasn't even worth signing up for the military. He tried to escape her mental, physical, and emotional abuse by leaving home and going far away, but her words followed him. He ended up in prison, with a dishonorable discharged from the military. After serving time in the military prison, he returned home to the same life and started the cycle on going to jail every so often. He did get married once, but that didn't last too long. He just ended up living a confused and angry life, always through misguided methods, trying to prove that my mother was wrong about him. He really went through a lot and lived that life that was spoken into his spirit.

Chapter 5 – *Darlene to the Rescue*

I may have had a few birthdays and gotten a little older, but my mom still had a tight leash on me. She still hadn't changed in the way she treated me, I still didn't feel or see the love that I wanted from her. My sister was still a part of the cheerleader squad, and was going places with them, but of course I could not go. I remember when my period came, and I was actually afraid to tell my mom because I didn't know if she would be angry with me or not. I did of course have to tell her, but it was like it was nothing to her. She got me the pads to use but that was it, she didn't teach me anything about caring for myself. I just thank God that there was Darlene, who was my best friend Lisa's sister. When I told Darlene that I had started my period, she sat me down and gave me the full run down on how to take care of myself during that time of the month. She talked to me about making sure that I was aware of my hygiene. She told me about the cramps, and how to take care of them as well. I was so glad for her being a part of my life. We actually grew up around her entire family so we called each other cousins. Lisa's family saw how I was treated differently by my mother, and they must have tried to compensate a little, and I thank God all the time for them being in my life. Back then, sitting with Darlene, Penny, Lisa, and Debra was good to my soul. Sadly, Darlene and Debra has gone to be with the Lord and they are missed and still loved. I now have Darlene's son Rico in my life because Rico mentors my son and loves him so much.

I continued on with school and life as normal as I could. I had known a girl by the name of Ann for a long time, and after a while, she became my best friend in the world. She would always ask me why I was treated differently by my mom. I would try to blow it off as if it was nothing but Ann wouldn't let me. She would always try to talk to me and tell me that things would be alright, so finally I felt at peace talking to her about it. Ann was my comfort zone; she was my strength away from home. Ann and I would sit outside with our other friends and laugh and play, but at the end of the day if no one else was outside, Ann and I would be on the porch talking about everything. I was too embarrassed to let anyone else know how badly I felt I was being treated but I think everyone already knew it, they just didn't want to bring it up. I remember some nights Ann and I would talk about so many things, her problems, my problems, and what we thought we could do to solve them. She would always tell me that God had a calling on my life because no matter what I went through, I'd always talk about the Lord in my conversations. I use to laugh at her and tell her God didn't have anything for me and she'd say that I would be ministering to people, and we'd just laugh. We were young teenagers talking about the Lord, and him having a calling for me. I could not see myself ministering into anyone's life! Ann would just say "Watch what I tell you!"

Chapter 6 – *Hard Working Man*

I wanted so badly to just fit in with everyone else. If I could have just traded places with my sister, I figured that everything would be alright. Everyone liked her in school, but I felt as if they looked at me like I was this dirty little girl who just so happened to live with my sister "Ms. It." I thought I could get some attention from my brothers, but my middle brother was always thinking of how he could make a quick buck, and the others were too much into themselves, so I was all alone trying to find my way. I could not blame them, they were like my dad in a way, and he was working all those different jobs so that my mom could stay at home and raise us. I remember my dad would drive dump trucks when he would be on his lunch break from his main job. Sometimes I would ride in the truck with him, and on the weekends, we would go to the incinerator. To me that was fun and it was real quality time. My dad wasn't the type of person who would say the words *"I love you"* to us, but he really didn't have to say it in order for us to know that he loved us. Not one of us felt left out or unloved by my dad, his actions spoke so much louder than his words ever could. The love he showed us was overwhelming and we loved it.

Chapter 7 – What's Done in the Dark Will Come to the Light!

Growing up with the understanding that relationships were not always exclusive took some getting used to. No matter how hard I tried, I could never quite get my mind around it being OK to cheat around on your significant other. I think we may have had one faithful person in our family that I can recall and that was my cousin Sandra. She was faithful to her boyfriend at the time, who is now her husband. While my dad was at work my mom had her affairs, and in due time my dad had his affairs as well. My dad had two daughters as a result of him being with another woman. I love my sisters Cookie and Donna very much. I didn't meet them until I was old enough to understand that I was not to go home and tell anyone else what I knew. I even met their family and they loved me just as I loved them from the beginning. I enjoyed seeing them because they always seemed to be happy to see me as well, and I felt wanted by them. It was what I had wanted all along from my sister that lived in the same house with me. I felt like she didn't love or care about me but my other two sisters did, and we became so close to each other.

My sisters' mom was always nice to me as well. She had other children, two girls named Katie and Faye, and a boy named Peter. They all made me feel like I was a part of their family. They never made me feel out of place and I thank them so much for that. I have nieces and nephews, great-nieces and nephews and I love all of them and they all love me so much. My children know all of their cousins because I didn't keep them away from my half sisters'. My mom finally found out about me having other sisters by my father when I was about twenty-three years old, and it was a mess. My dad had gotten sick, and my sisters' were going through some really hard times, and they needed my dad. My dad told them to come over because he was going to put an end to the hidden mess. They did come over and my dad introduced them to my mom as his children, and my mom flipped out. She had of course heard the rumors about my dad having other children but she never knew for a fact until that moment. She wanted to kill my dad with her bare hands right then and there, and if she could have, she would have killed my sisters too. My mom disliked the fact that I loved my sisters. She felt that it wasn't her infidelity or her hatefulness that pushed my dad out of the house and into another woman's arms, but rather it was just him being a no-good man.

This argument was between the adults, and should not have involved the children. For the record, we do not get to choose our parents, so all the children were dealt this same hand, except we had no input. Although my dad tried to make time for his other daughters, they missed not having him there to tuck them in at night, or waking up knowing that he was in the house with them in the mornings. In spite of all of those issues, he still gave them just as much love as he gave us. One thing that I can say about my sisters' mother is that she never made it an issue for my mom. She never tried to secretly let my mom find out about my sisters, or put my dad on child support. She knew my dad was a good man and a good provider.

Chapter 8 – *Giving Up The Cherry Pop or Did I?*

By the time I turned thirteen, I was starting to feel myself a little. My flesh was flickering and I had a certain type of craving going on inside of me that I didn't understand. I started to like boys, and started thinking about sex or at least the touching part of it. I had been seeing the person who would later become the father of my first two children every since I was a little girl. I knew that he liked me but I was afraid of boys at that time. I was however starting to have those feelings of wanting someone to touch me physically, but not so much sexually. It was more about me never really having the experience of touches in the house. There was no affectionate hugs and kisses from my mom. In my attempts to get that feeling of affection, I started sneaking around with John, and we would find places to kiss. I didn't want to go any further than that because I was just too afraid. On top of that, I could just imagine the beating that my mom would give me if she found out that I had let a boy touch me. So I would stay outside and play together with John and all of our friends. We had all known each other for years, so it was common to see everyone sitting together on the porch. My mom was very watchful and she knew that John liked me, so she did not like him at all. As time went on, I would sneak to John's aunt house with him and we would always do the touching and grinding thing, but no more than that. I was afraid of something going inside of me, but John would tell me that if I did it with him, he would be real careful. John was not a virgin, so a part of me felt like he knew what to do to make sure he didn't hurt me, but I was still afraid. As time passed though, I began to slowly drop my guard. He was really the first boy that I ever really paid me any attention so I had these little girl feelings for him. So much was going through my little head because I also knew about diseases and all those things, thanks to Darlene.

Nevertheless, I continued to sneak around corners with John and do the touchy feeling thing until one night I was out and I went and met him at his aunt's house. We were there alone as usual, and the touching and feeling started. One thing led to the other and the next thing I knew, I was undressed. I was so nervous, but the thought of someone finding me attractive enough to want to touch me really excited me. My sister had already been introduced to sex and was actually on birth control pills, so it was finally my time, and someone wanted me. He promised that he would take his time with me as he proceeded to climb on top of me. He was kissing me and trying to be gentle, but of course me being a virgin, the process was not a smooth one. It made me feel much better that he cared about me enough to try to make it right for me. He didn't get to fully finish what he had started because I was in a lot of pain and too scared.

I don't know if it was more the pain or because I didn't know the time, and didn't want my mom to come looking for me. He wasn't upset with me for having to stop because he knew that there would be other times for us to be together. We still did the touchy feeling thing but I made sure that I didn't go to his aunt's house again. always had an excuse because I think that he would have really made sure that he pushed his way through the next time and I would experience the thing that everyone had always talked about and that was the mythical notion of *'getting my cherry burst.'* I had felt the feeling of an actual penis, although it didn't fully penetrate me. I thought that I was the bomb and started to get a little wild. I began meeting other guys and in my mind, I wanted to be like that lady that I saw growing up with all the men. They made sure that she was taken care of, and didn't want for anything. I know now that I was too young to be thinking about that foolishness.

Chapter 9 - *Starting to Find My Own Wild Child Identity*

Although my sister was still very pretty and popular, I didn't think about her as much as before because I was finally getting my own identity and making my own friends. One day a lot of us were standing outside like we usually did, and we saw some new faces coming through our apartment complex. It was a group of guys that we had never met before, and when they saw us, they came our way and started talking to us. It was one of my cousins, my god-sister, my best friend, and I, and we were excited to talk to them. All of them had jeri curls, and thought that they were too hot. They were talking like they had just came from some 70's pimp movie. I had been around and heard so much game being pushed out by cheating family members, that I already knew how to throw conversation around just like they did. I already knew how to lie, look serious, and say I love you, knowing that I didn't mean it. After my early experiences, it came easy for me. These guys must have also underestimated me because I was very observant and most of what they said just rolled off of me. I just knew the more game they put out, the more game we gave back. I had just as much street sense as they did. It must have been easy because I wasn't looking for love. My mom had already told me that no one would ever love me anyway, and from the kind of love I saw, I didn't want that anyway. So the word love was just a part of the game along with lies and deception. We found out that the guys were new in town. Their families had been here for years but they finally decided moved here as well. They started coming around more often and talking to us. What we didn't know at first was that their families were big time pimps and drug dealers. There was about six of them in total, and they became popular in our area because they were the new fresh meat in the "Wee Wee" part of town, which is what everyone calls West Tampa, Florida.

I started to date one of them who was nicknamed Peewee. As strange as it was, my sister came out to participate in this one, and she was with Herbert and my god-sister started talking to Chris, my cousin Brenda was with Ross, and my other cousin Von was getting close to Vestin. We finally got them to tell us a little bit more about their lives, which I then began to investigate more into. I was excited because this kind of guy liked me. John got jealous because he started seeing Peewee and the rest of them come around and wanted to know what was going on. I didn't understand why John was getting upset with me; he was seeing a lot of other women, and acting very whorish. He would tell me that it was Peewee who was whorish, but I didn't care, I'd seen enough cheating, and lying, so it didn't matter, I just rolled with the punches, I didn't know anything about real love, although I wanted it really bad. I was just getting wild and having fun, so I wasn't concerned about anything or anyone who wasn't helping me achieve that. Peewee and his crew would come around to Vicky's house because her mom was away from home quite a bit. She would just leave Vicky at the house and we would always tell my mom that we were at Vicky's. She actually lived right across the streets, so could just call us at any moment or look out the door and see that we were over there for real. What she didn't know was who was in the house with us. So we'd be over there till late and my mom didn't mind. John was still tripping because someone else was stepping on his toes. I guess he figured that the new guy would step in and finish what he had started. I had been seeing Peewee for a few months while John was sleeping with everyone he could get to sleep with him.

One night I ended up at Vicky's house and everyone had coupled off and were in different rooms. That left me alone with Peewee an empty room. I hadn't had a chance to touch and feel with him to feel his size through his clothes so I was just unsure. I was already reading a magazine and eating peanuts to distract him in hopes that he wouldn't ask for sex, but he did and we went into the room and laid in the bed. I refused to put the magazine and peanuts down and he was cool with that, he was going to do it anyway, so I laid down braced myself preparing to feel the final pain of what John had started. To my surprise, it didn't hurt at all and it was over quick. Peewee got up and said "well damn you read a book and ate peanuts while I got that." I was still looking crazy because then I felt like maybe John had broken the main mold and Peewee finished it so I was good, I was no longer a virgin.

Chapter 10 – *Let's Party and Have More Sex*

I was still seeing John every now and then and finally I did give him the opportunity to go ahead and finish what he started. I started sleeping with John more often, because Peewee would always be out of town. He wasn't my boyfriend anyway, so it was alright. Knowing what I knew about John, I was still being with him unprotected, and I ended up getting a sexually transmitted disease from him. My mother really hated him after that, and I could no longer hide that I was sexually active. Mary was another one of my friends that was like a sister to me. Mary would also sneak around with my brother and they were supposed to be play sister and brother!

I started being allowed to go out as long as I was with my sister and god-sister. My sister still had her special friends that she would deal with on her own time, but I was a reason for her to be able to get out the house and she took advantage of that. We would go to this club called The Alien. I was growing up, and had a little figure by then. I was about fifteen or sixteen years old and meeting so many new guys. I was still on and off with Peewee, but he was still back and forth out of town with his family. I didn't fully understand the life of a drug dealer, but he was always in and out of town. So while I was out, and able to do what I wanted, I was wild and very promiscuous, even in my conversations. I met this guy named Lefty that bothered me every time he saw me out. Sometime I'd go by his mother's but I'd never sleep with him or anything just mere conversation and trying to run game like I had it going on.

One particular night I was at The Alien and I saw Lefty, and he asked me to ride with him. We went to pick his friend up from home because he wanted to come to the club as well. While we were waiting for his friend to get dressed I went to sit Lefty's room with him, and he started to touch me. I actually got a chance to feel Lefty's penis through his pants and it was bigger than what I felt with John and I immediately knew in my mind that I was not going to sleep with him. I'd heard my mom say many times that you never let a man with a big penis man just jump up and down inside you and damage your body. I knew that he would not be someone who would be jumping up and down inside of me. Lefty kept trying and I kept telling him no, and then he forced himself on me. I yelled and screamed, and fought but I was embarrassed because his friend was in the house and he had a girl with him. They did not think that anything was wrong with what was going on so I just held the screams in. Lefty proceeded to take me and I'd never felt so much pain in my life. He didn't hold any punches; it felt like my entire insides had burst and was in flames. It almost felt like my body wanted to go into shock just to numb the pain I was feeling. This was the first time that I'd had sex and saw blood. He wasn't gentle at all and everything was sore. After he climaxed, he kissed me and went to take a shower. He brought me back a towel and kissed me again, and told me to go clean up so we could leave. I began to think to myself if I had somehow told him that this was alright to do, or if I made it seem like I was cool with this painful shit. I was confused because he didn't act like he had done anything wrong. I knew that it was my big mouth, and those conversations that had led me to right where I was. The bottom of my stomach felt like it was about to fall out and I was so ashamed. It was so obvious but the girl and the guy sat quietly because they had just had sex as well, and they were loud too, but they had already finished by the time that we came out. It felt like I had been in there for hours with him. I went in the bathroom and cleaned up, and just wanted to get back to the club with my sisters. They didn't' even realize that I had left the club. I left so quick and thought I would be right back, but that man could have killed me and no one would have known that I had left the club with him. When I got back to the club, I acted as if everything was fine. Vicky did ask me where I went off too, and I told her that I rode with Lefty to pick up his roommate. I never told anyone about what really happened that night until right now. The truth is that Lefty raped me that night. I was more careful now with my choices of going places with men, even the ones I knew. I continued to run into Lefty at the club but I always went the other way.

Chapter 11 – *You're So Devilish*

Things had begun to change for me at this point. My 'Mother Gooden' said that I was a devilish little thing. Guys would watch me and see that even though I had many friends around me, I was really a loner. No one knew my business or whatever I did because that part of my life was between me and God. I only told people what I wanted them to know and didn't say anything else. People could guess all day long, but I wasn't into explaining myself to anyone. I knew that people were going to say or think whatever they wanted to anyway, and for the most part, I didn't care. When it came to relationships, I would do whatever I had to do in order to get that man. It would be by any means necessary, and I learned that from watching and listening to my mom. I was starting to have so much fun, and enjoying the process of becoming a woman. I really didn't care about men or their feelings so I was just doing whatever. I was still seeing Peewee in an unofficial capacity, probably because I had gotten close to some of his family members, so he was just the extra that came with seeing them. My sister stopped seeing Herb because she knew he was seeing other women. I even ended up meeting one of his other women, and we actually became very close. Those guys were not my sister's cup of tea anyway, she always went high class. I was afraid to go too high because I didn't want to get let down, and so I stayed in my comfort zone in terms of the types of guys that I got involved with. We all continued to hang out and my sister went back to hanging with her own friends again, which actually set well with me because I didn't want her in my business anyway. I wanted to do what I wanted to do and I wasn't extremely excited about having my sister around me, imagine that. I still felt certain vibes by my sister and knew that there was this competition thing going on. I never wanted to compete with her because she was my sister and I loved her, although Ann and others people use to tell me that they didn't like how she treated me and that I was just as pretty as she was. I don't think that I ever believed them, and felt like they were just trying to make me feel good about myself.

    I started hanging around more drug dealers and pimps, but I still had time for Ann and all the other people who I was friends with. At that time I didn't have a lot of female friends, but people like Ann and Vicky would forever be in my life. Mary was out doing her own thing and we saw each other every now and then. I still saw John every now and then partly because; I was close to some of his family members. There was a group of guys that we knew; they formed a group called Gamma. It was Sir Miguel, Kathartist, Sir Curls, Roe, Carl, and a few others in the group. Vicky, my sister, and I always pretended that we were the lady Gamma's. We hung around with them for a little while but it didn't last too long. We were having so much fun, mostly being around nothing but men. Kathartist and Vicky continued to see each other even after the other ladies stopped hanging around their little group, and she ended up getting pregnant by Kathartist.

Chapter 12 – *Pimps, Hoe's, Sex, Drugs, and Loving It!*

My cousin Brenda and I became really close, we did everything together. At the time, Brenda was dating one of the guys who was a pimp and a drug dealer. By then, my heart and mind was covered in stone, and to a degree my flesh was as well. That was my protection; it was a way of not allowing anything or anyone to hurt me again. I still went by the mantra that my dad would tell me, "Never let the devil see you sweat or cry." I did my best to make sure that I wasn't in a position where anyone could even try hurt to me. Brenda and I ended up getting a place together and we lived the fast life. With Brenda having a boyfriend who was into drugs, we were like a safe place for him to operate out of. We had all of our bills paid for us, but we also had to have dope in our house that we kept for him. We even started transporting dope for them on occasions. I had begun to sell weed, rock and powder cocaine. I also started drinking, but when that wasn't enough, I decided that I'd try to snort some cocaine one night. I was scared at first, but I thought, 'What the hell', so I did it. Actually, I didn't get anything from snorting like other people did; I was just doing it because I was there. I tried to smoke a little weed but that gave me a headache so I left that alone. I guess I was at a time in my life that I was going to just do what I wanted to do for me. I didn't realize it then but now I know that I was just covering up many of the unresolved pains and hurt that I had felt in my life. All of the drinking, the sex, and just all out partying was just the mask. I acted as if I didn't have a care in the world.

Brenda still worked a job, and sometimes she would come home from work on her lunch break. I'd be cooking and having a party and we'd just call her job and tell them that she had family emergency and she wasn't coming back, so that she could stay there and party with us. I'd see Peewee when he came in town but for the most part I was hanging with his family. He was doing his thing out of town and by then I didn't give a damn. I was doing my thing with all of his family members. Peewee tried to be abusive every now and then, even going so far as to act like he was going to hit me. He tried to treat me like I was one of his women who were out there in the streets, trying to bully me. I remember one time in particular, he did hit me and, I lost it right there in his mother's house. I tried to scratch his eyes out of his head, and when my brother got a wind of what happened, he came and was going to have a shoot out with Peewee. I had to beg him not to do anything crazy because even though we had a big family, they had one too. I knew that I was still going to be around Peewee and his family so I didn't want him to come and try to protect me from people who I would ultimately be back around anyway. I felt like I handled it well myself.

Chapter 13 - *Look at Me, I'm Important, I'm Somebody Now!*

After some time away from him, I began to find myself around J.C. a little more often. He took me under his wing, and I started taking his ladies to the stores to get their trick clothes. I also had to get ice, and other things to put on their faces when the big man beat them up real bad. John wasn't the only player that I was around; there were other people who I worked with. I was making all kind of runs, going back and forth to Miami, Sanford, Belle Glades, and Ft. Lauderdale and wherever else I needed to go. Most of the time we travelled with a man we called Crow. He was like our personal body guard. We didn't have many issues with people because they knew that we would only have to make one phone call, and either 'Short Arm Mike,' Crow, or Billy would come running to our rescue. Brenda and I would be driving around in Eldorado's like it was nothing. It use to hurt John so much when he saw me driving their cars. I had gotten the reputation that I was one of their women, but that didn't bother me at all because I didn't care what people thought.

Sometimes I would go to the corner with them, and my friends would see me, they would slam on their brakes looking at me crazy, but I'd just laugh and still hang out there kicking it with the ladies. I didn't care what people said, if I could endure my mom, then I could handle anything. Some days it did cross my mind to get out there with them to see if I could do what they did. I remember when John said to me "Girl I need you to realize that your black ass has something that not many people have or know what to do with. You are a full fledge whore!" Of course I was about to curse him, but he explained that a whore was born but a prostitute was made. He said you had to teach a prostitute what to do, telling them step by step until they learned. When you were born with your shit he said, then that's your blessing, your tool to life. So when that "pimp" told me that, I was good to go. I had a tool that could get me anything I wanted if I knew when to use it. I was ready to go to work because for some inner reason, I knew when I was with a man, I was on my job!

Chapter 14 – *The Girl Got a Little Talent Too!*

I started sewing clothes, and in fact, I would sew most of Brenda's and my hot clothes. I would venture to say that although we lived a dangerous life, sewing for me was that peaceful place. At that time I just felt like I could do whatever I was big and bad enough to do. Even with that attitude, I still prayed, and I guess that's why God watched over me during my ignorance. Brenda and I enjoyed going up to this particular restaurant every night to eat and just socialize with everyone who was there. We were in chill mode.

John use to tell me that I had better be glad that I lived in Tampa, because otherwise he would put me out there on the 'Hoe Stroll.' He used to say that to me because I was real fly at the mouth, I didn't give a damn what anyone said or thought of me. I'd curse them out real bad and be ready to fight. Brenda was always a little scared for me because of the way I spoke to J.C. She thought that at times, I just talked way too much. I had to let her know that John wasn't my pimp and I didn't take orders from him. She just figured that because his women were all deathly afraid of him, coupled with the fact that I was talking shit to him in front of them, he would eventually do something to show them what happens when someone gets a little loose with the words around him. I had to tell her that I wasn't worried, and that he actually said he admired my boldness. Even his women would ask me how I was bold enough to talk shit to him. I told them straight up, "It's all of you that work for him. I don't, and he does not run me!" On top of that, my brother was doing his thing as well, and they knew each other.

Through it all though, I just really enjoyed being around all of them. It gave me something to do as well. The girls enjoyed me being around, and it made me feel wanted. Behind all of the tough words, the shit talking, and hell raising, I just wanted to be loved and accepted. I hadn't forgotten about my old friend Ann, I would still pop in every now and then to check up on her to make sure that she was alright and didn't need anything. Brenda and I still had our lives outside of hanging around them. We would date 'regular' type guys and do a lot of crazy things together. We never thought that hanging around the people we did would cause us a problem until one day Brenda and I was at Ben T. Davis Beach with some friends. We were grabbed by some guys who pulled us deep into the water and told us that they were going to kill us because of the people we dealt with. For whatever reason, they decided against it, and they let us go. When we got out of the water, we made a phone call to tell of what had just happened, and soon the beach was full of people with guns. They were looking for the men, but they were nowhere to be found. 'Short Arm' Mike said that he had a feeling he knew who it was and that he would deal with it. That should have been a clue that we were probably in over our heads, but even that didn't stop us from hanging around them, and still being crazy. God was truly watching over us even in our ignorance.

Chapter 15 – *The Word of God Will Always Follow You Little Girl!*

Peewee's mother and his aunt were loving, saved, Christian women, and they loved me. Every time I went to their home, they would always try to talk to me, to pray for me, and anoint my head with oil. They would also tell me to get away from their family because I was a good girl and I needed to be saved. His mother also told me that I was loud and needed to learn how to quiet my voice. I learned so much from Ms. Sheridian and my mommy Gooden, but I wasn't ready to pay any attention to them at that particular time. I enjoyed when they prayed over me and told me that God had a calling on my life, and that I was different than the rest of them. It was another chance for me to feel like I was being noticed, and that I was someone important. I ended up getting really close with his family; I got to know all of the people who were really in charge of the 'family business.' I actually started dating other people in his family and acted as if it wasn't anything. I had seen it growing up in my family, so for me I guess I didn't have the normal reservations that other people may have had, I was just climbing the ladder to get what I wanted. I made it up in my mind that I wasn't going to stop either, until I had reached the top. In the end, my goal was to make sure that I didn't need of want for anything.

Every now and then I'd see John and we'd talk but he

didn't like the life I was living. My dad didn't like it either because I had dropped out of school three months before graduation. I've always told people that I dropped out because I wanted to run the streets, but the real reason is that I was afraid to take the final test. My mom had already put it in my head that I would never amount to anything so subconsciously I felt like I my mom was right so I went with that out of fear.

I wanted so much to finally please her that a part of me accepted that I was black, ugly, and that no one would ever truly want me. I was afraid of taking the test and failing, so instead of going forward and taking the test, possibly passing, and then be happy, I took the fearful way out and left school. I felt like the men who wanted me was enough, even if it was just for sex, it felt good enough to get by for the time. I felt like I was making something out of myself so I didn't need a diploma to confirm it. I felt loved, and it was something I always wanted to feel. Because I didn't know what real love felt like, anytime someone gave me attention, I associated it with love. It felt like I was living the song by Tupac, and the verse went "and even though I sold drugs, they still showed a young brother/sister love." I felt that street love.

By now I'd met Peewee's step mom Mable and I also met Chips, and oh how I loved those two women. I was hanging with them more and going to Belle Glades, Florida all the time. What I didn't know was that J.C. and Mable didn't really get along well with each other, but that had nothing to do with me. They would argue over cars and almost anything else, it was crazy. I think it was the fact that he didn't like the Jamaicans that Mable hung around with while his brother was locked up. There was a time that Mable, Chips and I headed to Ft. Lauderdale, where Peewee was, and he and I argued the entire time I was there. I know he wanted to hit me, but he didn't because he probably knew that between Brenda and myself, we would have probably kicked his ass to sleep. Every now and then when he came to town he would always put out those petty threats. His act of dominance tickled me because I knew he was a pimp and too cute to fight. I was really just giving him his ground and making him feel that macho shit with me. To be real though, I would have gotten with his ass had he hit me wrong!

Anyway, when Brenda came home for lunch that day, I wasn't there. Because the trip was all of a sudden, I didn't get a chance to talk to her. She called Kim to see if she had heard from me, and Kim told her that I was in Ft. Lauderdale, and that she was about to go there as well, so of course Brenda didn't go back to work and jumped in the car with Kim. Brenda was very protective of me. She made it to Ft. Lauderdale and I was so happy to see her. We hung out for the first couple of nights and then it was time to head back home. We lived so dangerous because no one knew when we came or left out of Tampa but God was there even in our ignorance.

Chapter 16 – *Choosy Lover*

When we got back in town, the battle between J.C. and Mable continued. I dropped Mable and Chips off at their spot and Brenda and I kept the car. We went riding around and checked in at home. I went by J.C.'s place and he noticed that I was driving the other Eldorado. He asked me where Mable was, and wanted to take the car from me. It wasn't to be mean to me but to be mean to her. It was in fact his brother's car. They always had this tug of war thing going on with what belonged to Big Herb, and I just happened to land in the middle of it. J.C. got in the car and started throwing all of Mable's Jamaican cd's out the window. I was telling him to stop because she left me responsible for the car, but he said to tell her that he did it. After his tirade, I was able to get away from him with the car. I had to call Mable and tell her what happened, and after I did, they had a big arguing match. J.C. was asking me why I was even around Mable, and she was telling him that he didn't own me. She told him that she was like a mother to me and that I wasn't one of his whores. J.C. then had the nerve to tell her that I had picked him and wanted to be with him, which tickled the hell out of me and Brenda. Mable asked me what the hell was his problem and was I whoring for him. I told her of course not, and then she wanted to know about his claim that I somehow had chosen him. That was a funny choice of words because I didn't belong to anyone but myself! From that day forward, Brenda decided that she would call me *'Choosey Lover'*!

That situation finally blew over for the night and things went back to the normal hustle and grind by morning, and I sure was glad. The next day when I saw J.C., and he started going on about how I had chosen him, and I had to step on that real quick. He didn't pay my shit talking any attention any more than I paid him any attention. Not only did Brenda name me *'Choosey Lover'*, she also called me Reba Shayne from the daytime soap Guiding Light, because she knew I wasn't scared to run through the entire family. I thought that it was cool at the time, and although I didn't literally go through the entire family, I did have my share. If we didn't hang out with them at the house, then we would meet them at different hotels, just to clear our heads from all the hoopla that was going on at the other houses. It's also the place where I would sometimes put meat on the girl's eyes. I would make sure that I had enough lunch meat to be able to put it on their eyes after J.C. would have beaten them half silly for whatever reason, and sometimes for no specific reason at all. We enjoyed going to the motels on Nebraska Ave. until they started shooting in the area. We had to stop going over that way, and ended up going to hotels over on Hillsborough Ave. We would hang out there and get some rest, snort some drugs, screw or whatever we felt like doing at the time.

Chapter 17 – *Ouch, Was That a Spirit Speaking Out From The Past?*

My life was so wild and although this may sound crazy, I was classy with my wildness. I didn't get involved with guys who could not do anything for me. I was only interested in someone that had something to offer me in one way or another. I didn't hang with any other women other than Brenda, Vicky, Ann, and Lisa, so it was mostly hanging with guys for me. I loved listening to music and dancing, I wanted the music to be loud, so much so that it would continue to drown out the voices in my head that came back to haunt me quite often. These were the voices that said to me that no one would ever want me, and that no one would ever love me, and that I would never amount to anything. Those words were always cutting me like a knife, and like the bible says, tongue is sharper than the sword, and those words always cut deep down inside of me. Whenever those voices came up in my head, I wanted to dance to drown them out. I would snort powder, take a drink, I had even started smoking weed as a way to escape the voices. Sometimes I would even lace my joints with cocaine. I just wanted to always be numb, but at the same time, I wanted to be numb with pain. I wanted to assure myself that someone wanted me so I'd put myself in certain positions to be around a certain group of big money men just to see how they'd respond to me and they always would because I knew how to talk to a man, I knew what to say to drive a man out of his mind. Whether it be in the bed or out, for the most part. I could meet a dude, sleep with him, and if I wasn't satisfied, I would go sleep with someone else that same night. *I thought I was caring about me but I really wasn't, I was hiding behind my past hurts and pains.* I just felt like I wanted pain. When I say that I wanted pain, if a man penis wasn't a certain size, he better know what to do with what he had because I needed to feel pain. I know it's crazy as hell, and even after my mom said don't let a man with a big penis jump up and down in you, I was already so accustomed to pain until pain was all that I knew. It was all that I wanted in order to calm me down. It was almost like a pacifier for me. It didn't even have to be pain physically; I also prepared myself to receive pain emotionally, mentally and sometimes verbally. Verbally however, I gave it back blood raw. My mouth was so raw; I would say some things that would make anyone male or female fold into a fetal position. Now that side only came out as needed though.

I was still hanging with the same people, still selling powder and crack cocaine. I learned how to cook dope and use to do that as well. So I was selling the same stuff that I was using. More experienced users told me that I was doing it all wrong. They tried to show me how to do it correctly, and I was just following the crowd. I didn't snort with just anyone;

it had to be other ballers or people spending big money. Some nights we'd sit up and snort and I'd be the first to fall asleep with powder hanging out of my nose. I would hear everyone laughing, telling me that I was wasting money. They were woke all night, so I guess they were snorting correctly!

Chapter 18 – *Just Where Do You Think You're Going!*

Times were getting crazy for the people that I had been hanging around, and it was about time for the most of them to relocate and get some new wings under them. Everyone was preparing to head out of town to North Carolina. Brenda and I wanted to pack up and leave as well, so we all met at the Motel on Hillsborough & Florida Ave. where we were supposed to leave at a certain time. Brenda and I wanted to go out before we left but J.C. told us what time everyone would be pulling out and if we are not there when it's time, we would get left behind. It was crucial that they leave at a certain time in the middle of the night and that it was important that we knew if we missed the ride, no other ride would be coming anytime soon. We said that we understood, and then called a few friends to come get us. So we went out anyway, and when we returned to the motel, we found out that they had really left us, just like J.C. had said they would. They took all of our bags out of the room that had all of our clothes, a photo album lots of pictures in it, many without anything on. So Brenda and I had to walk all the way back home and figure out which way to go in life since they had left. We had just missed our meal ticket. Well it was by the grace of God that we were left because they end up getting busted. It was like a domino effect, they all started going downhill, getting Federal Prison time. Some got life; some got twenty years, while some even died in prison. Brenda and I still had our place, and we let my brother move in with us for a little while. We started hanging with people like Chris, Fabby, Red Man and Capone. We stayed in that place until we couldn't pay the bills anymore so we moved out. I had also started seeing this guy name Bennie, who I truly fell for. Bennie had someone so I had no intentions on getting serious with him but he held himself in a different way and believe it or not, he liked me and he didn't like hurting me. In the end, that is exactly what he did though. He allowed me to fall in love with him, and even my family fell in love with him as well. Strange that a man that who didn't want to hurt me, hurt me the most by loving me.

Chapter 19 – *Back to Those Familiar Spirits, Didn't See It Coming*

I ran back into John and we started talking again. He was still just as whorish as he always was, and to be honest, so was I, so I tolerated it because I was still doing my thing as well. John ended up giving me a disease again and my mom was furious because I had to go the doctor that she had us going to for years. To make matters even worse, my cousin Pat worked there. Now it was that, or go to the health department. I did end up going there once, and that was the most shameful thing in the world to me at that time. Not knowing when to say no, I continued sleeping with John, and got pregnant by him with my first child. He was living back and forth between me and his other women. I sometimes would stay with him at his mother's house. As time went by, my life was taking more crazy twist and turns. I had stopped the snorting, but I was still drinking all of the time, even while I was pregnant. I was trying to keep that bandage that I had on my life from falling off, I didn't want to expose everything that I had been hiding for so long, but it was finally being torn off, and that open sore that I never allowed to heal was just as raw, still as sore as it had always been. I guess the pain was still fresh because even when I was out hustling and I'd go see my mom and dad, my mom would still tell me that I was stupid because of the people I was hanging with. She told me that I would end up going to prison for the rest of my life because I was with dangerous people. So no matter what I did, even when I didn't ask for anything, to her I was still this dumb and stupid little girl. I was never good enough for her.

So much had begun to change in my life, Brenda met a guy name Michael and started seeing him and moved on with her life. I'm not sure what happened, but Brenda and I stopped talking. I heard that she had gotten pregnant and she and Michael got married. With my self-esteem at an all-time low, I was still messing around with John who had already gotten another girl pregnant, and supposedly had about three other women pregnant at the same time. I allowed so much to go on in my life because no matter what I did, I would always fall back into the pattern of always having a smile on my face but dying on the inside (**SILENT SCREAMS**). I missed my life with my other extended family and it was like I got a hard life reality check. They were gone, even though I still had contact with a few of them; it wasn't enough to keep my life going as it was. The funny thing about I was that I knew that they didn't make my life better, I just felt like being around them I felt like I was untouchable. With them, I was somebody, and now I had found myself back in the rut that I came out of. I was severely depressed and settling for the same shit all over again. I felt like I had nowhere to turn!

Chapter 20 – *You're About to be a Mother*

The months were passing by with John and me looking forward to having out first child together. It would be my parents' first grandchild from their daughter. My brother had gotten a girl pregnant but was uncertain if it was his baby or not. John cheated the entire time I was pregnant and I continued to have my fun but I wasn't sexual with anyone while I was pregnant.

When it was time for me to deliver, I was actually drunk when I went into labor with my baby. After the delivery, I went to my parents' house to live with them, and in spite of my mother's hatred for me, she liked my son. She also knew that I didn't know anything about how to raise a child; I was still trying to figure out how to deal with myself. I knew one thing though, I didn't like the way she treated me as a child, so I was going to do my best to be a better parent to my child than she was to me. I was eighteen years old with a baby, and wasn't quite sure what I was supposed to do. It was a new experience, and at first it was exciting.

It wasn't so much the same for John because he had kids already from so many other women that it wasn't even funny. I just wanted someone to love me, but I seemed to be looking for love in all the wrong places. I was at a point in my life that I was looking for love in a man, in sex, and wherever else I could find it. Those were my *silent screams*, but no one knew about this because it didn't show in my face. Ann may have known, but she was the only one. On top of everything else that was going on, John's mother Lillie tried to deny my son because he was darker than his other kids, even though my son looked just like his mother. I didn't care if she claimed him as her grandchild or not, it really didn't matter to me. It wasn't like she was doing anything for him anyway. I felt that as long as my daddy was going to be in my child's life I was OK. I was just always afraid and hoping that my mom didn't try to treat him the way she treated me. I just never understood why she hated me so badly.

Chapter 21 – *You're a Lying Wonder, You Never Loved Me, You Lusted Me!*

Through the years I had plenty of men say they loved me, especially John. He would always tell me how he loved me, but I didn't believe him because it's hard to receive those words as true when someone was giving you diseases. From what I learned, it was his usual line he told every woman he slept. He was always telling them that he loved them, just to get them in the bed. He wanted to run around and be with any woman he could, yet wanted all of the women to be faithful to him. It's clear that someone wasn't being faithful to him because he kept coming back with diseases all the damn time. I got into it with one woman but that was brief because I didn't want to be arguing with another woman especially over a man that was definitely not good. I had already seen the infidelity drama play itself out growing up. I didn't want to continue the cycle even though I was deeply in the process of keeping it going. I felt parents, and especially mine were supposed to love each other, but with the kind of the infidelity that I saw, there is no way that there was any kind of real love there. I began to use the word I love you also, since it seemed to get people what they wanted. The word love was just a game to me to get me what I wanted. I didn't believe a man could love me, so when a man said those words to me, I took it as just him starting to play his version of the game.

I do believe that in the end, after all I had endured, and after being there with John through everything that I went through with him, he finally began to slow down. He was getting older and settling down a little more but by then I didn't give a damn. I was being faithful but not because I was in love, but more because I just didn't have the desire to mess around with anyone else at that time. No one caught my attention enough to shake me like that. So John and I ended up moving to a place on Columbus Drive and things were alright but he still had his cheating moments, and after a while, so did I. Even though he thought that I was the most faithful woman that he had, I honestly may have actually have been the worst. I ended up flipping the script on John with my feelings. I didn't want to feel for him anymore; I wanted that numbing pain again so it was time to rear my head up and look from side to side to see what was out there.

John and I met one of the guys that lived a few doors down from us, who was also a drug dealer. We began to get involved back with selling again. With both of us now selling drugs, we would go to West Tampa and sell our drugs, and then come home for the night. I got pregnant again, and had a daughter this time. My first son was living with my parents at the time, and she would always tell people that I didn't want my son or I that I had given my son to her, so I could run the streets. In actuality, I did not give my child away. After I had my son, I mentioned earlier that I went to live with my parents. When I moved, it broke their hearts that I left with my baby.

My mom tried to be slick, and every day after she got off from work, she would come by my house and ask if she could get the baby for a little while, and of course I would tell her yes because I was trying to hustle anyway, so that was good for me. When I would go to pick him up, she would already have bathed him and had him ready for bed. She would ask me to just leave him because it wasn't good for him to have been wet and taken out in the cold so I'd say yes and she would bring him to me on her way to work the next morning. When she got off from work, she would stop by again and ask for him, and the same thing would happen. I would get there to pick him up, she's say that she had bathed him, and that I should let him stay. I started to realize it was a pattern but I didn't say anything because it' worked well for me. I was selling drugs and running wild, but then she started talking about me, saying I didn't want my baby so I went and took him from her and she begged me to let him stay again, saying she'd bathed him and I told her I didn't care, give me my baby. Around midnight, I got a knock at my door, and it was my dad. He had come to tell me that my mom could not sleep and asked me not to do that to them; he said that the baby had given both of them a sense of peace between each other. For my dad it kept him busy because he's the one that actually took care of him, and for my mom, she had a baby around. She enjoyed anyone or anything that was helpless and needed her.

So that night I packed him a bag and sent him with my dad, but I told my dad how bad my mom hurt me by telling people I didn't want my child. I was allowing them to enjoy their grandchild, and it was helping both of them. They got to have their grandchild around them for their own personal reasons, and it gave me time to hustle. So once again the routine started, she would bring him in the morning when she was on her way to work and come by and get him on her way home. Some days I would tell her not to give him bath because he was coming home with me period. The routine started to happen so much until that it just became the way it was. Even today my son is still living with my parents and he's in his mid 20's. Unfortunately, when he got older, my mom started doing the same things to him that she had done to me. She had started calling him dumb and saying that he was stupid and ignorant, and that he would never amount to anything, just like his mother hadn't. While it tore me down, it motivated him in a different way. He was determined not to let her get to him.

Chapter 22 – *Now You're the Mother of Two and Still Messed Up!*

My daughter was now here and I didn't want to let her go for the world. John's mom Lillie again questioned if my daughter was his child because she looked Colombian, which was just like her crazy ass actually. As time went on, she actually became very attached to my daughter and wanted her all the time. John and I was still selling drugs and even keeping some of our neighbors stuff for him when he would go out of town. By the time he came back, we had cut his shit up so much that it was unreal. He either knew it and didn't say anything or he just didn't have a freaking clue, but either way we made plenty of money off of his stuff when he left it at our house. I figured at the time that I wasn't just going to be keeping other people's stuff in my home for free, and when my doors get kicked in, then it's our asses going to jail, and you are at home looking at us through the window. One evening, we were sitting in the house, and we saw cars pulling up from every direction. We heard a loud noise and saw that Manuel had just gotten busted. I was terrified, and ran to get John. I told him that we needed to flush Manuel's shit and we started flushing, but vice ran right past our house so I stopped flushing. I stayed in the bathroom with the drugs and waited for John to tell me to flush or hold off. After John said that the coast was clear, we saw Manuel and all his women get escorted out of the house, and into the waiting police cars. As he passed us, he said that he was gone for good. I was sad because he had become such a good friend, but then my mind said, "Oh shit, we still got a lot of his shit, and it's come up time!" I wasn't going to take him anything or call anyone and mess around and get cased up. So we made the best of the situation, and this was a win-win situation for us. We had product that was purely profit for us, and in the game, it doesn't get better than that!

Not long after Manuel was gone, John started acting like a fool again. He was sleeping with the different crack heads that were also his customers. Eventually, he started to use the drugs as well and lying about it on top of that. He tried to hide it for the longest time, but in all things, time will tell you everything you need to know. One particular woman claimed that he had gotten her pregnant as well, but he denied that child and said that she was just a lying crack head. Funny thing is how he was also lying to me about using crack, but he was calling someone else a lying crack head. The child did turn out to be his, and she looks just like him and could be a twin to my daughter. This wasn't anything new for him though, he had already pulled this before. He had gotten one of my neighbor's pregnant right after I had my son, and we were living in the same complex with my mom. He even denied that child until the truth came out. She looks identical to my daughter as well.

So for the most part, John was just that nasty dog type of man that wanted to just run around. I still kept quiet for the most part, and allowed the hurt to just fall on me because again, I felt that at least someone wanted me, and according to my mom, I should have been glad at that fact. John did get a regular job, and I was picking up his check every Friday, I also had the car more than he did, and I started running things around the house. I wasn't doing it to hurt him, I was doing it to help him because he started using drugs, I would take his money and pay the bills, take care of his car and the things that he needed handled. I never took his money and just did what I wanted; it was always for the good of the household. I was really getting tired of John, the women and just life itself, so although I had the two kids, I thought that realistically that I could do bad all by myself.

Chapter 23 – *Time to do Something Different and Still Do My Thing*

I had finally had enough of his doggish ways, and put him out. He went and stayed with other women as always. Although we had two beautiful kids together, that still wasn't enough to make either of us want to stay because we still wanted to continue to experience all of life's pleasures without being tied to one person. We were both hustlers and trying to keep it as real as we could. He had started using drugs again, and lying more, and of course he was already a cheater so things were at the perfect point in time for us to end it. I also wasn't letting him touch me because of the drug girls that he was sleeping with, so I figured that it was time to go my own way, and that's just what I did.

I moved to duplex that was closer to my parents place, and that's where my daughter and I was comfortable and content. My son was still living with my parents by now, so I was starting to venture out a little more. I could always take my daughter to her other grandmother, you know the one that didn't think she was hers at first, but finally wanted to have her, so she could take her around talking about how my daughter looked just like her. I didn't' care, my daughter loved her grandma and it gave me that free time to do me. I could sell drugs and not have her around it.

So I was hustling as I always had, and had gotten back in

contact with Brenda, and we started doing our thing once again. This time though, we were much older, and much wiser, and she had to be more discreet because she had a husband. Michael even hung out with us every now and then as well. I guess he wanted to see what I was all about. Sometimes I would even go by their place, just to hang with them. Then I started doing other things that I had done in the past, and that included snorting drugs. I would hang out with the girl who lived next door to me named Patrice, who was hustling as well, and we would literally cut the fool together. She had her spots, but mine were usually going to the Double Decker and Manila to make my money. It was so funny to me because not too many people knew what I was doing because I had a certain clientele, and I didn't mix business with pleasure. If I went inside the club, I made sure I wasn't dirty. If I was going to hang out for a minute I made it a rule to never close the club, staying there until the lights came on.

If it was business that led me to the club, I wouldn't go inside; I'd stay outside, handle my business, and be out. I didn't like a lot of direct full attention. When I went places I'd always come after the fact and leave before it's over. I've always liked the darkness.

Chapter 24 – *I Need Some Attention, So I Guess I'll Dance!*

It was getting rather dull in my life; I was doing the same things day in and day out. I had a friend named Kim who was dating a man by the name of Sammie. He had women that danced for him, and I was interested. I was in search of attention, so being the quiet attention getter; I thought dancing might just fill that need. Even though I always silently compared my body and looks to other women, I always felt like they looked better than I did, and I hated competition. To me, you just had to figure out a way to win, so I would go to practice dancing with Sammie and the other girls. It was fun because I've always been very limber and could put both of my legs behind my head and do all kind of crazy things with my body, so that made dancing even better for me, especially if I had a drink in my hand. My body was looking and feeling better feeling because I had stopped snorting. I realized that I was just wasting my time and money. I thank God that I didn't know how to snort it right. What people had once laughed at me about probably saved me. It just wasn't meant for me to get that stuff down my nose like it was supposed to go. Now I was still drinking my Hennessey, but not the other stuff like I would drink back in the days of Bulls, MD22, Wild Turkey, or Private Stocks. Now if I drank a beer, it had to be ice cold and either a Michelob,

Ice House, or Bud Ice. Although I didn't stay with Sammie long, I started modeling lingerie and bathing suits, and from there I did a couple of dances in the local clubs but that wasn't my cup of tea so I started doing private dances. Sammie actually set up a few of the dances. Through those dances, I got more connections and started going to Miami to dance as well. I was doing dances on the water in the yachts for a lot of rich Colombian and Italian men. Every now and then we'd get a rich white man to call but most of them where very old and just wanted to get their freak on. Some of the girls would get paid more because they did more. I wasn't about to be sucking a penis for extra money, and they were not going to be sticking their penis in me for any amount of money. I didn't knock them for what they did because I knew for them it was all business, but just was not my type of business. I enjoyed doing the private dances. I also did a few personal dances and got more money for allowing the old geezer to touch my butt or put the money directly into my clothes. Even if it was just into my bra, or panties, that just turned them on. I was a big tease and I knew how to tease an orgasm out of them and still walk away without being touched. As long as I had a good drink in me, my ass would dance all night. Some of the girls still did pills, powder and everything else but that wasn't for me. I made the money off selling them powder when they wanted it.

Chapter 25 – *Seeking Out My Victims!*

Not many people knew that I was dancing, selling drug or using, so this may shock some. While that's one side, the other side is that some may think that I was worse than what they may be reading. There were many rumors floating around that said I was on drugs because my kid's father had started using. It still didn't matter to me what people thought. I use to be out on Main St. at Boogies, a place called Night Lighters before it shut down, the Zanzi Bar and the Station Bar. I would be with Mickey, Fat Mike, Chris, Ole Man, Otis, Amp, and Big Dre before he was killed, and many others. I rarely went inside of any of them because that just wasn't my thing; I was always outside the bar, observing and seeing who I wanted to be bothered with that night.

I was good at getting what I wanted most of the time. If I had an attraction to a man, then I would watch him just like men do to women. I would see what he was like, learn his characteristic and see how the women are up around him. Once I had learned enough, if he was what I wanted, I would go for it, and 9 times out of 10 I got it. My main goal was to watch the men that thought they was so big, the men that thought their shit didn't stink, and had women chasing them and begging to be with them. Those were the men I wanted. I wanted to get with them and turn them completely out and then walk away from them. I wanted to see them when I wanted to and not give a damn about them. I didn't hold any punches either. I wanted what I wanted and I went after it and I made sure I gave it my best. I never gave any of them the best of me, although they felt that's what they were getting. Once I had my first time with them, I would string them along how I wanted to. I might see them the next day and maybe not even speak or contact for weeks. If I felt like the job that was done in the bedroom wasn't what I wanted, I would not contact them anymore unless I felt like it. When they would see me in the streets, I'd make excuses, but for the most part I was very blunt in the bedroom, I'd tell a dude quick, if he didn't perform like I wanted, then his ass was history because I pretty much knew my game was tight. I never got involved with guys who talked too much. That was another reason I watch my prey as I called them, but I wanted to see if they were busy body ass men because there are some men out there that talk more than women, so I needed to make sure that my game was top notch, quality and kept under the rug.

I use to hear that it was always good to get involved with someone that had someone because then you don't have to worry about them running and telling because they would only be telling on themselves. I respected that game as well but that wasn't always my target because on real, I didn't want the next woman's man and I didn't want a dude that everyone else had been with. I always went behind the scenes, and some would say that the dude must have kept me behind the scenes. If I were to ever call out names, it would knock the feet from under a lot of people. Some guys wanted to be seen with me but I said no. I felt like I was a go getter, I'd take care of my family by any means necessary and whatever it took to get down with my man to make shit happened, hey I was that chick, but only if I liked you like that, or I would play dumb. I made so many guys think that I was in love with them and cared so much about them, but if they tried me I would sleep with their brother, son, daddy, or whoever I felt like sleeping with just because I could. I thought I was making them feel and look bad, but the reality was that I made myself look bad. My sexual nature was always on the rise, so it was as if I could have sex all day and night and not think twice about it!

Chapter 26 – *Family Secrets AGAIN*

Every now and then I'd run into my oldest brother while I was out there on the streets. We would hang out together and I knew that he was out there doing his thing, and he knew I was doing mine, but to us it was all just a game. My brother ended up getting crossed up, and had to do time in a federal prison. I knew that the only real communication that I could have with him was through writing, so we wrote to each other every now and then. Our letters were pretty vanilla in the start, we would talk about what was going on, who was in, and who was out, what was the word on the street, all of that stuff that was just things that filled the letters up. Then, we got on a serious topic, and he wrote to me, and told me that he hated my mom. I never told anyone about these letters between my brother and me. It was just between us, because I wanted to be able to really talk to him like never before. I told him that I figured he hated her because of the pain she caused in his life. He told me that the pain was more than I imagine. As we wrote to each other more and more, I told my brother that I loved him so much and how I use to cry silently when she would beat and make fun of him. He said that he didn't understand why she was so mean to him, and that he didn't understand what he had done to her. I couldn't answer him because I felt the same way, I didn't understand why she was so against the youngest and the oldest child. I had heard some years back that the man who raised me as my father wasn't my actual biological father. At the time I didn't want to hear that kind of foolishness because he was the only father I knew, the only father that I wanted, and the only father I would ever have.

Again I was faced with one of those *silent scream* moments out of fear it may have all been true. I didn't want to mention it to my dad so I talked to my middle brother about it and he claimed that it was just a joke that he had made up long ago to mess with me. I finally sat down with my dad one evening, and we talked about the issue. He told me that to him, I was his daughter no matter what anyone said, and that he loved me more than anything. He said that if I wanted to get tested to learn the truth, then he would do that and no matter what the test came out to be, he would still love me the same. I told my dad that I wasn't going to talk to him any more about that mess. He was my father, and that was that. So I told him that I didn't want to talk about that subject again in my life. It still crossed my mind if that was the reason why she hated me much. I do know that the man who was at the other end of this mystery had always made comments to people that I was truly his daughter; he even told his children that I was their sister. I did find out many years later that the only real father that I knew was indeed my real father. He had gotten sick, and had to be in hospitalized, and they needed to give him some blood transfusions. The nurses started talking about the blood types and that was the day that my dad and I secretly found out that he was my biological father, and I praised God for that!

That still leaves my oldest brother with so much anger inside that he did not know who he could talk to about it. I was there for him and we talked about the many secrets that we held between the two of us. He knew about things that had happened in his own life and I had the things that I had from my life, and then we had those things that we both had recollections of. We never told anyone about the things that we talked about, it was our secret. It seems like I have always been able to talk to him when no one else could get through.

Chapter 27 – *Let's Have More Fun*

Well I ended up talking to John again, after all I did see him all the time when he would come to get our daughter and take her to his mother's house. He was rarely able to get my son because my parents loved that kid and didn't want him around John and his family. My mom took the position that if John's mother felt that my son wasn't her grandbaby, then she should keep her ass away from him. I didn't question my mom's decision on that because I felt it would have only made problems worse and she may have mistreated my son. John knew I was still doing my thing and he jumped in a little but I was still watchful of him because by now he had been with way too many women to count. I could not really say too much to him because I had done my thing with many different men as well. I wasn't going to be putting myself in harm's way of getting a disease.

So that part was definitely a no go. John's brother had a girlfriend that I'd been knowing for a while but we didn't have a close relationship because she hung out with the girl that John was cheating on me with. Once they stopped being close, Brina and I started hanging out together. When you talk about fun, Brina and I had so much fun hanging with my cousin Al, it was ridiculous. We would hit that interstate back and forth to St. Petersburg, just doing our thing. I won't get into Brina's or Al story because that belongs to them. I will say however, that we were nothing nice together. The three of us hung out so much, and it would not have to be anything planned, it could be at the spur of the moment, but whenever it was, we would get it going. Even when Al wasn't there, Brina and I hung together strong and hard.

Chapter 28 – *Girl You Still Live Dangerously*

My brother and I had started working together. Yes, it was the middle brother, the one who had been a hustler from a child. I had the guns and drugs stored in my house and that was my fault because I already knew that you did not lay down to sleep where you shit, and not only was I there, but I had my child laying in the same shit. On one particular night, John and I was about to go out. We were going to take our daughter over to his mother's house first. I was in the front room, and he was still in the bedroom. Then suddenly we heard a loud noise and I ran into the living room to see what was going. I was shocked to see someone coming into our house with guns. We were being robbed by the *'jack boys.'* These were the guys who robbed nothing but drug dealers because nine times out of ten, they knew that the people they hit would not be calling the cops, it was all a part of the game. They came in and grabbed us, and put guns to our heads and started asking us where the drugs and money was hidden. We kept telling them that we didn't have anything on us. I look back now and see just how foolish that was. They started looking all over the house, and made John get into the bathtub. He was still talking shit and wanting to fight but it was too many of them. I kept telling him to be quiet and just do what they said so they can leave. Then one of the guys who was in the room with me, put the gun to my daughter's head and asked me where the drugs were. I told him that I didn't have any drugs there, and that they were making a huge mistake. I told him that we didn't keep any drugs in the house, and that this was our home.

They knew that my brother and I worked together so they figured that we must have had a stash at our spot. Now they did find the guns but they want guns, they wanted the money and the dope. They had me strip off all my clothes and one of them put his finger up inside of me to fill for drugs, and once he didn't feel any, he pulled the gun away from my child's face. She was actually playing with the gun and the dude told me that he would not hurt my baby if we just told them where the drugs were. I kept telling them that we didn't have anything in the house. Finally one of the dudes came from the other room and said "Damn Mick, you told us this girl had dope man ain't nothing in here motherfucker!" I knew right then when I heard the name Mick that this was not a random event. This was done by someone we knew but I couldn't say anything. Mickey turned and looked at me through his mask and then they all they ran out. I did call the police to tell them that someone had broken into our home, but that was in order to get a police report, so the landlord could fix the door. I couldn't tell the police why they broke in because when you're doing dirt, you have to realize that it's a dirty game and you have to charge things like that to the game.

The crazy thing about the entire situation was that I had just got a new package and I had so much dope hidden right in the room that they were looking in, but they didn't find it. A few days later reality slapped me across my face and said ***"You damn fool, you had guns pointed at your family, even your daughter, and you didn't give the dope up. You could've gotten your entire family killed in the house and the dope was right there!"*** So that was seriously a lesson learned. I had a part of me that also knew that if they would have found the dope, then they would have had to use those guns on us because they would not have taken a chance on leaving witnesses. It would not have made sense to have the heat of murders, and not have gotten anything in return, so while it was a dangerous gamble, I knew that if I would have given them a reason, they would have taken care of all of us that night. After the incident, I called my brother and we talked about what had happened. We continued on doing what we did, but I secured my doors better. I also learned that I had better keep my guns on me, even though it probably wouldn't have made a difference that night because had I fired, it was still about five other guys with them, so I know someone would have gotten hurt bad. So between my brother and me, we charged it to the game and we kept it moving.

I continued to hustle and dance for a little while longer,

and would hang out with my cousin every now and then. We would go riding sometimes just to see what was going on. She was dating one of John's friends named Darren, and we would get their cars and just ride so we could wild out with them some nights. Every now and then we'd go through College Hill and we would run into this guy that I knew when we were younger. I never paid any real attention to him, but we would be friendly and speak when we saw him. Every time we would say hi, he would always try to give me the eye, but I didn't' pay it any attention. He definitely didn't care that I was with John because he was still trying to talk to me. It was almost as if I could not go there without running into him. Even when me and my other god-sister G.G. hung out, we would see him. I did see him at a few clubs, and I would promise to meet up with him or tell him that I was coming back to see him but and I never did. I just never felt that it would go anywhere. He was very attractive and I liked his swag but it still wasn't enough to get me to move towards him. I do admit that he was on my list, and I was sizing my prey up, but I was just uncommonly hesitant when it came to him for some reason.

Chapter 29 – *Same Ole Games Man, Come On*

Things were beginning to feel like I was stuck in a bad episode of my favorite show. I enjoyed certain parts of my life, they were exciting, but then other parts were still stuck in that rut. If you can imagine having your favorite meal on the table before you, but with it, you have old and dirty silverware, and the plates are nasty. You want the food, but the extra stuff just kills the excitement, and so you can't focus on how much you want that meal because of what you would have to go through to get it. I mean John was still up to his usual stuff, after all of those years. He was still trying to sleep with as many women as he could. At some point you would think that a man would grow up, and start thinking with his other head, but not this one, he was going to be a dog until he died. I wasn't feeling him anymore like I use to, I had already made the move to be by myself once before, but this time it was different. I wanted to move forward and find out what was out there for me. I wanted to raise my kids, and keep it moving. So John and I officially broke up for real.

This was not like all of the other times, when it was breaking off, this was really us breaking up and letting it all go. I wanted to allow all the women who he wanted to sleep with, to have him. So I put his stuff out and he came by with his cousin, and they got everything out of the front yard. I locked my door and let them load the truck and it was a wrap. John and I went our separate ways, and it was hard at first because it was just the company that I was missing, I wasn't missing the man anymore because he hadn't played that roll in a while. Now I can't take it away from him that he was always been a hard worker, he was just making crazy decisions, and he wanted every woman in the world. It was tired of watching him get diseases and in my mind I figured that it would be AIDS next, and I wasn't trying to have that so I got out of that line of fire. I also didn't catch any more diseases because I was no longer sleeping with him. You would think that going through all of this would be enough to be the entire story, but this was only the beginning!

........To be continued

Preview from Part II

From Book Two *"Someone Almost Loved me To Death"*

.... and he would walk through the door after a long night of doing drugs, and being with his women in the streets. He would come over to me, and for no reason at all, punch me in the face. Every night I had to get on my knees to take his boots off. If I did not go fast enough, he would place one foot on my thigh and use the other foot to kick me backwards. The only thing that I was allowed to do was to get up and continue to take them off. After I would finally get them off, I had to take off his clothes and perform oral sex on him until he told me to stop. Some days the inside of my mouth would have blisters. I also had to follow him through the house because he hallucinated a lot when he was on the drugs. I had to look through every room to assure him that no one else was in the house. If I made one wrong move he would punch and kick me until I folded up like a baby on the floor. He would sometimes get scissors and cut my clothes off because he thought I had been with other men and that I was nasty. I was too afraid to even cry.

Someone To Love the Little Girl in Me

www.ingramcontent.com/pod-product-compliance
Lightning Source LLC
Chambersburg PA
CBHW060402050426
42449CB00009B/1870